Original title:
Botanical Ballads

Copyright © 2025 Creative Arts Management OÜ
All rights reserved.

Author: Gabriel Kingsley
ISBN HARDBACK: 978-1-80566-695-0
ISBN PAPERBACK: 978-1-80566-980-7

Garden Whispers

In the garden, veggies plot,
Tomatoes giggle, beans are hot.
Peas in pods have quite a laugh,
While carrots dance with leafy staff.

Bees are buzzing, quite a tease,
Tickling petals with the breeze.
Sunflowers wink, the daisies chuckle,
As rabbits sneak snacks, oh what auffle!

Lullabies of Leaves

Leaves sing softly, rustling cheer,
Telling secrets, lending ear.
Dancing shadows under trees,
Swaying gently with the breeze.

A clumsy squirrel trips and rolls,
While lazy worms just dig their holes.
The tulips sway, they giggle mild,
For every bloom, they feel like wild!

The Secret Language of Petals

Petals whisper, gossip flow,
Roses boast, but violets glow.
Lilies tease with perfume sweet,
While daisies play at hide and greet.

Wildflowers wear their colors bright,
Gossiping through day and night.
Sunset brings the fireflies,
They join the dance beneath the skies!

Symphony of the Swaying Stems

Stems are swaying, marching tight,
With daisies twirling, what a sight!
Grasshoppers leap with laughter loud,
While sleepy bugs form a cozy crowd.

The flute's a feather, quite absurd,
As chirpy crickets sing the word.
Mossy stones, they tap their feet,
While flowers sway to this sweet beat!

Echoes of the Evergreen

In a forest of trees, oh what a sight,
Pine cones falling, much to their delight;
Squirrels chatter, they dance with glee,
While branches tickle each other, you see.

Moss spreads jokes on the forest floor,
Whispering pines say, "Give me more!"
Bark beetles laugh, with a twinkle in eye,
As the echoes of laughter bounce up to the sky.

Lullabies of Leaves

Leaves rustle softly, a giggle in wind,
Tickling the branches, the laughter won't end;
A clover sings sweetly, a cheeky little tune,
While daisies make wishes upon the bright moon.

The acorns are planning a wild little spree,
Dancing with shadows, as bold as can be;
Whimsical vines weave tales by the hour,
Of plants that can talk, and trees that have power.

The Song of the Sunflower

Sunflowers sway, with smiles so wide,
Feeling like dancers, full of pride;
With each little spin, they cheerfully say,
"We're the stars of the garden, hip-hip-hooray!"

Bees buzz around, a buzz-worthy sound,
They join in the chorus, full of joy unbound;
With petals that shimmer, it's quite a scene,
As they sing 'bout the pollen and what might have been.

A Garden's Grief

Oh, the garden weeps for its lost little bugs,
Who ventured too far, and got caught in the rugs;
The weeds hold a funeral, wearing their best,
While roses reminisce of the bugs they loved best.

The soil tells tales with a groan and a sigh,
Of critters who laughed, then said their goodbye;
But daisies remind them with petals so bright,
That laughter leads on, even through the night.

Melodies of the Moonlit Orchids

In the garden, they dance and sway,
Orchids giggle at the moon's soft ray.
With polka dots and stripes so bold,
They whisper secrets never told.

Petals twirl like a silly hat,
They laugh at the presence of a passing cat.
Each bloom brushing up against the night,
With twinkling laughter, oh what a sight!

The Rhapsody of Roots

Deep in the soil they wiggle and squirm,
Roots have a party, oh what a term!
With dancing fibers and gnarled embraces,
They share their tales about hidden places.

They gossip in whispers beneath the ground,
Of worms who twirl and dance around.
With a raucous laugh, they keep it neat,
Swaying in rhythm, beneath little feet!

Hymn to the Hidden Ferns

In shades of green, they softly croon,
Ferns giggle under the watchful moon.
With fronds that flutter like a fan,
They whisper jokes—it's quite the plan!

A leap, a stretch, they tease the breeze,
Hidden secrets dance with ease.
Golden spores, a sprinkle of cheer,
These ferns know how to spread good cheer!

Ode to the Blossom's Breath

A flower's breath, oh what delight,
Tickles the nose, such a whimsical sight.
Petals puffed up, like balloons they float,
With silly scents, they tease and gloat.

In gardens they laugh, with colors bright,
Mixing hues and sharing light.
Whispering sweetly in the sunny glow,
Blossoms always put on a show!

Silhouette of the Silverbell

In the garden, flowers sway,
Silverbells dance in disarray.
Bees with hats buzz all around,
Chasing raindrops that hit the ground.

Worms wear ties, oh what a sight,
As they wriggle, ready for flight.
Ladybugs grin, they steal the show,
Critters gather for this toe-to-toe.

A Dusting of Daisies

Daisies bloom, a curious crew,
Painting the meadow with laughter anew.
Winds play pranks, tossing them high,
Some get dizzy, oh me, oh my!

Grasshoppers leap, trying to mime,
The wiggly dance, oh so sublime.
Sunflowers giggle, heads in the air,
While roots gossip, with the freshest flair.

The Fertile Fable

Once a seed with dreams so grand,
Planted in soil, oh, so bland.
It sprouted tales of mighty trees,
And whispered secrets to the breeze.

But then came showers, quite a show,
Making mud pies where the flowers grow.
Beetles rolled like they were bold,
Claiming treasures of greenish gold.

Reflection in the Rosebush

Roses blush in a curious way,
Plucking thorns on their glamourous day.
A mirror pond showed them their style,
They posed and laughed for quite a while.

A squirrel critiqued with a flick of the tail,
"Points for color, but where's your detail?"
Petals fluttered, a haughty waltz,
As they threw shade, oh how they'd pulse!

A Harvest Hymn

In the garden at dawn, gnomes dance with glee,
Dressed in hats made of leaves, just wait and see.
Tomatoes wear sunglasses, fresh out of bed,
While carrots trade jokes, feeling quite red.

Radishes giggle, their tops all a-twirl,
Peas in the pod shout, "Come join our whirl!"
Pumpkins plot mischief, they're rolling around,
With cornstalks as dancers, they twirl on the ground.

Bees buzzing loudly, they join in the fun,
With flowers as partners, they dance in the sun.
Squash does the cha-cha, quite out of control,
While the lettuce laughs hard, now losing its roll.

When twilight descends, the crickets then play,
They serenade veggies, in their own quirky way.
As stars fill the sky, the harvest sighs low,
With laughter and mirth, let the good times flow.

Wandering in the Wilds

In the forest, oh what a sight,
A squirrel's dance, quite a delight.
He thinks he's slick, but oh so wrong,
Tripping over roots, he's lost his song.

Under leaves, I spy a rose,
With a sign that says, 'Please don't pose!'
Its petals blush, as I burst in laugh,
A flower pouting, not a photograph.

A cactus jokes, 'I'm prickly cool!'
While daisies giggle, 'What a fool!'
They play hide and seek, toss all their woes,
With nature's whimsy, as humor grows.

The wilds abound in silly tricks,
Like bees in bow ties doing their kicks.
In this garden, joy's not far,
For every bloom shines like a star.

Shadowed Blooms

In the shade where shadows creep,
Lurks a bloom that's lost its leap.
With wilted dreams and a droopy grin,
It says, 'I'm just waiting for gin!'

The violets chuckle, quite high-strung,
With puns on petals, they're well sung.
'Why do we always stay so blue?'
'Because laughter fades when it's past two!'

A dandelion, proud and bold,
Tells tales of wishes, never old.
'I've seen the sun grow tired indeed,
But I still plant my giggle seed.'

In the corner, a lilac spills,
With laughter thick as springtime frills.
These shadowed blooms beneath the sun,
Show that life's a joke, let's have some fun!

The Fragrance of Ferns

The ferns stand tall, with a swish and sway,
One whispers, 'It's good to play!'
With leafy games and ticklish tease,
They shimmy about in the summer breeze.

A wise old fern gave me a tip,
Watch out for squirrels, they trip and slip!
Their nuts roll far; it's quite a scene,
Chasing after acorns, oh so keen!

With a wink, the ferns start to sway,
'Let's have a ball, or maybe a play!'
But then a rabbit hops in surprise,
With a leafy crown and gleaming eyes.

So here in the patch, laughter grows,
Where ferns hum tunes and friendship flows.
With every rustle, joy extends,
In the fragrance of ferns, let laughter blend!

Shimmering in the Shade

In shady spots where sunlight fights,
A daisy giggles, 'What are those lights?'
Is it a firefly dressed in gold?
Or maybe just gossip from the bold?

A hydrangea musters up some pride,
Claiming its past as the floral guide.
'Though shades may shift and colors change,
My humor's bright; it's never strange!'

The shadows dance, a comic play,
As sunbeams join in, come what may.
Everyone here has a role to spin,
In this quirky world, where chuckles begin.

So if you sit in the dappled gloom,
Expect a laugh, or two, to bloom.
For shimmering moments, shades reveal,
A plant's whimsy, oh what a deal!

The Orchid's Embrace

In a garden bright and spry,
Orchids twirl and dance nearby,
With petals soft they flirt and tease,
While bees buzz by with utmost ease.

They wear their colors—pink and gold,
Like party clothes; they're fun, not old!
As stems entwine, they giggle and sway,
In the sunlight, they laugh all day.

A thistle said, "You think you're grand?"
Orchids shrugged, "Just take our hand!"
The daisies sighed, "We'll join the spree!"
And thus began their wild jubilee.

So if you wander past that way,
Find flowers joking, come and play!
For in this bloom-filled, vibrant space,
Laughter grows with every trace.

Ode to the Olive Tree

Oh mighty tree with twists and bends,
You stand so tall, as if to send
A wink to all who wander near,
With leaves that rustle, cheer to hear!

Your olives hang like little moons,
While squirrels hold their secret noons,
They nibble bits, while branches sway,
A snack attack, in bright display!

Sometimes you sigh, your bark in pain,
But then you chuckle in the rain,
"Water's good for the soul! Don't you know?"
You stretch your limbs, put on a show.

So raise a glass of olive oil,
To celebrate your timeless toil,
For every twist and quirky knoll,
You make the world a joyful scroll.

A Song in the Succulent

In pots lined up, a squad of green,
The succulents stand, shining sheen.
With prickly backs, they hum a tune,
And under lights, they dance by noon.

They've got a groove, they've got a beat,
A spiky flash mob on their feet!
With rosettes and plump array,
They certainly know how to play!

Cacti giggle, "We've got spines!"
"Please don't poke, just bring the vines!"
While jade leaves whisper, "We're divine!"
Each blushing bloom, a show of shine.

So if you seek a leafy jam,
Just drop on by, you'll feel the glam!
For in this crew, the joy is real,
A succulent song that you can feel!

The Cormorant's Canopy

Underneath the greens so lush,
The cormorant lands with a splash!
With wings outspread, he's quite the sight,
In leafy layers, he takes flight.

"Oh me, oh my!" the branches sigh,
As he dives deep, and flies on high.
"Can birds dance?" a nearby fern asks,
As cormorants twirl in aerial tasks.

"Just watch me glide!" the cormorant brags,
While ferns reply with leafy jags,
"We sway in style, our dance is slow!"
"Try a flip!" "Oh, no, not in the show!"

So here they flourish, tree and wing,
In nature's theater, they all sing!
With laughter echoing through the trees,
Join this party, capture the breeze!

Verses from the Vineyard

In the vineyard, grapes do slide,
They dance on vines, with nowhere to hide.
A waltz of flavors, sweet and bold,
With laughter and giggles, the stories unfold.

The barrels chuckle, tickled with wine,
While corks pop off like rockets, so fine.
A grape jokes with a playful stare,
'I've got a punchline, but I'm just too rare!'

Sipping and slipping, the sun sets low,
Wineskin tricks play, putting on a show.
The wind shares a secret, a vintage tune,
As leaves shimmy lightly beneath the moon.

So down goes the harvest, lively and loud,
Each grape a member of a jolly crowd.
Pour out your heart, let laughter arise,
In vineyards where humor and nectar surprise.

Legacy of the Larch

Oh larch, my dear, with needles and laughs,
Tell tales of squirrels and their silly paths.
You stand so tall, sturdy and sly,
With branches that wave as the birds go by.

In autumn's blaze, you wear a crown,
While acorns drop like a jest from a clown.
The forest giggles at your grand retreat,
As leaves twirl down to a whimsical beat.

A breeze tickles bark, as if it can tease,
'You're looking good, swaying with ease!'
Your roots spread wide like its own dance floor,
Where every critter finds joy to explore.

The legacy grows as seasons declare,
Laughter will linger in the crisp air.
With a wink to the sky, you sway and you sway,
The larch knows how to brighten the day.

In the Shade of the Sycamore

Beneath the sycamore, shadows take flight,
While critters giggle at a squirrel's fright.
The breeze whispers jokes, soft as a sigh,
As leaves shake their heads, oh me, oh my!

'Knock, knock,' says a cicada, full of cheer,
'Who's there?' chirps the grasshopper, quite near.
With a buzz and a chirp, they create such a ruckus,
In this leafy theater, nobody can hush us!

Under thick branches, the laughter stays warm,
While daisies debate the best weather charm.
A ladybug rolls, laughing so crude,
'Flowers, you're cute, but I'm in the mood!'

With each windy jest, the sycamore groans,
As squirrels collect bits of acorn loans.
In a belly of green where giggles abound,
Every whisper and rustle is merrily found.

Moonlit Moss

Atop the moss, beneath the moonlight,
Frogs sing their songs, creating delight.
They croak out their wishes in comical tune,
With fireflies dancing, they light up the dune.

In the cool of the night, the mushrooms advise,
'Take life with humor, and don't wear a guise!'
Toadstools nod softly, as laughter spills free,
A rollicking show, just for you and me.

The moss whispers secrets, tickling your toes,
While crickets share tales of their hilarious woes.
You'll chuckle at shadows that frolic and tease,
In this whimsical kingdom, we laugh as we please.

So here's to the night, where the humor is rife,
Under soft glowing lights, let's enjoy our life!
In a patch of fresh moss, we'll share every cheer,
With a grin on our faces, there's nothing to fear.

Secrets of the Strawflower

In a garden where secrets weave,
A strawflower tied up in a sleeve.
It giggles at bees that try to pry,
Whispers of pollen, oh my, oh my!

A waltz with the wind, oh what a sight,
Dancing away from a bug in flight.
With petals of yellow, it struts and sways,
Chasing the sunlight through laughable days.

Little critters gather to play,
Strawflower tells tales in its own way.
With humor and charm, it spins a yarn,
Of sunny skies and midnight charm.

So if you find joy in petals so bright,
Remember this flower, and take delight.
For in every bloom, there's laughter to share,
Secrets of nature, floating in air.

The Scented Sonnet

In a garden filled with scents so grand,
A sonnet was penned by a flower band.
With roses that giggle and lilies that blush,
Each verse perfumed in a fragrant rush.

The daisies burst out with a comic plight,
As violets argue who smells just right.
While thyme chimes in with a cheeky rhyme,
"Oh please, oh please, we're all in our prime!"

The breeze carries laughter, it flits and flies,
While humor unfurls in the colorful skies.
A banquet of scents and a hearty cheer,
Together they sing, bringing us near.

So if you should wander through this delight,
Join in the laughter, share in the light.
For blooms and their verses, oh what a ton,
In the scented garden, there's always fun.

A Tangle of Tansy

In a patch of lunacy, Tansy sits tight,
With leaves that are tangled, a comical sight.
It twirls with the daisies, both giggling with glee,
Joking with dandelions, "Come dance with me!"

Each stem tells a tale of ridiculous woe,
About spills and thrills, and the neighbor's crow.
With whispers of mischief, it plots a good laugh,
Creating confusions, a botanical path.

In the midst of it all, a bee buzzes by,
With a wink and a nod, it's a cheeky fly.
A tangle of laughter, where blooms intertwine,
A party of petals, oh isn't it fine?

So gather your friends, don't be shy to dance,
In Tansy's embrace, give humor a chance.
For every good flower has stories to bust,
In the tangle of greens, bloom joy and trust.

Blooms Beneath the Stars

At nightfall, the blooms begin to giggle,
Under twinkling stars, their petals wiggle.
Geraniums toss back their heads in delight,
While nightshade pulls pranks in the moonlight.

Jasmines are whispering secrets so sweet,
As lilies juggle pollen to the beat.
Foxgloves are sharing a mischievous grin,
Under the laughter of night's soft din.

A dainty bouquet floats on an unexpected breeze,
Bringing forth chuckles from all the trees.
In this garden of whimsy, they sing and they play,
Where laughter and blooms dance the night away.

So if you gaze up at the stars above,
Imagine the blossoms in a chorus of love.
For under the night sky, with humor so vast,
The blooms beneath stars share joy unsurpassed.

The Poesy of Petal-Soft Clouds

In the garden, daisies dance,
A bunny prances, it's a chance.
A ladybug plays the tambourine,
While a gopher tries to keep it clean.

The sunflowers wear a silly hat,
Whispering secrets with a chatty cat.
The clouds above, like cotton candy,
Tickle the leaves, all feeling dandy.

A bee can't find his way to tea,
He's buzzin' 'round a tall pine tree.
The roses giggle, their thorns hold tight,
To catch the breeze and take flight.

While the grasshoppers start a band,
With lilting tunes, so sweet and grand.
In this world where whimsy reigns,
Nature's jokes will drive you insane.

Whims of Wisteria

With wisteria vines swaying low,
They twist and twine, a lovely show.
A squirrel sports a tiny hat,
And grins while doing the acrobat.

The tulips tease the shy old bee,
"Come play with us, don't just flee!"
Marigolds are painting the town,
With laughter bright, we wear a crown.

A gnome with mischief in his eyes,
Decides to wear a pumpkin disguise.
The wind plays tricks, with petals in tow,
As daisies gossip, "Did you know?"

In this fest of colors and mirth,
Each bloom creates its own rebirth.
With whispers and giggles, we all join in,
For every flower is born to grin.

Fables of the Flora Found

In the forest where the wild things grow,
The ferns hold secrets, don't you know?
A hedgehog boasts of his spiky crown,
While mushrooms dance in their polka gown.

The daisies plot to make a cake,
With raindrops sweet, for goodness' sake.
For every bee that drops a note,
A ladybird writes, "Let's have some hope!"

The violets argued who's the best,
In shades of purple, they took their rest.
But giggles floated through the night,
As fireflies flickered, sparking delight.

With tales of whimsy under the stars,
Each flower holds laughter like treasure jars.
These fables spin in twilight's glee,
As nature's choir sings out, "Join me!"

A Tapestry of Thorns and Thistles

Amidst the thistles, rose a jest,
A thorny crown put to the test.
The ants march in a funny dance,
While daisies' sway leaves us in a trance.

The prickly pears exchange sweet words,
As hummingbirds hum happy chords.
A clumsy toad hops, lands quite wrong,
Creating a scene that's hilariously strong.

A cactus dreams of being a tree,
"Just wait," it sighs, "You'll see me free."
With laughs that echo in the sun,
Each spiky friend wants in on the fun.

So let us share in nature's play,
Where thorns and thistles brighten the day.
In this tapestry, so full and bright,
Even prickles can sparkle with delight!

The Lush Lyric

In a garden where daisies danced,
A snail on a stroll had a wild chance.
He slipped on a leaf, oh what a sight,
Chasing a sunbeam, with all of his might.

The roses were laughing, full of delight,
As they teased the old willow, who shivered in fright.
A bumblebee buzzed by with a tune,
Claiming the petals were his afternoon boon.

Tulips in bow ties, so dapper and neat,
Rambled on gossip about bees and their sweet.
While violets giggled, their whispers so sleek,
Sharing the secrets of the garden's cheek.

And in this lush land of bloom and of cheer,
Every plant told a tale, every bud had a sneer.
So let's raise a drink, to the fun we've all had,
In a world of green friends, nothing feels bad!

Emerald Embrace

In a pot sat a cactus, quite grumpy today,
He rolled his green eyes at the sun's bright array.
"Why do you shine when I'm stuck in this spot?
I'd wiggle and jiggle if I could, but I'm not!"

Next to him, a fern fanned with flair,
Said, "Don't be so prickly, just brush off the glare!"
They plotted a scheme for a wild little fling,
To dance in the moonlight, oh, what joy it would bring!

A chive with a giggle, said "Come join my band,
We'll make garden music, just follow my hand!"
Lettuce joined in, with a sway and a spin,
Every leaf adding laughter, each moment a win.

So off went the friends, through the stars and the grass,
As daisies stood tall, cheering on the class.
With green hearts united, they swayed till the dawn,
In their emerald embrace, all worries were gone!

The Journey of Jasmine

Jasmine, the jester, in a gown of pure white,
Took a trip to the woods, under the moonlight.
With aromas cheerful, she danced on a breeze,
Chasing down fireflies as light as the leaves.

She met with a thistle, who spouted wise tales,
Of prickly adventures and stormy gales.
"Don't fret little flower, for thorns can be sweet,
It's laughter that matters, not woe or defeat!"

Then jumped a bold daisy, with a wink and a grin,
"Let's spread joy around! Yes, let the fun begin!"
They twirled 'neath the stars, with giggles so loud,
A whirl of sweet petals, oh how they were proud!

For the night was alive with the joy of the game,
As blooms shared their stories, even nettles felt fame.
With jasmine leading, through fields lush and free,
They painted the night with their wild jubilee!

A Chorus of Chrysanthemums

A chorus of chrysanths all gathered one day,
To belt out a tune in a bright, flowery way.
With petals all polished, and scent in the air,
They practiced their notes without worry or care.

The sunflowers chimed in, with a melody bold,
While pansies and violets added their gold.
Oh, what a ruckus, a riot of sound,
A symphony blooming from ground to ground!

Then came a rogue lilac, with notes slightly off,
His quirk made them giggle and teeter in scoff.
But every voice mattered, in harmony's game,
For laughter and music were their claims to fame!

As dusk settled down, they sang one last round,
With petals all shaken, joy softly unbound.
So join in the chorus when flowers convene,
For fun is their language in forests serene!

Echoes in the Herbarium

In a dusty old room, leaves dance and sway,
Herbaceous whispers have plenty to say.
With tales of the thyme and the sage's grand plans,
They giggle and chuckle in leaf-covered bands.

A cactus spoke up, oh so prickly and proud,
"I'm the coolest plant here!" he bellowed out loud.
But succulents snickered, their greens ever bright,
"Chill out, dear cactus, you're spiky, not right!"

When fungi join in, they start to debate,
Mushrooms say jokes that are really first-rate.
"I can mushroom for fun!" one said with a grin,
But his spores all fell down with a comedic spin.

In this herbarium, laughter does bloom,
With jars filled with plants, we banish the gloom.
So next time you wander where the wild herbs hide,
Listen for giggles; the flowers abide!

Dance of the Daffodils

Daffodils twirled in a sunny parade,
With petals like trumpets, their bright music played.
"We're the stars of the garden!" they cheered in delight,
While daisies rolled by, in skirts shining bright.

In spring's merry ball, they showed off their flair,
"Watch us, we shimmer!" they waved in the air.
But violets moaned, feeling slightly outmatched,
"Come on, we'll bloom first, though your prance feels unmatched!"

A worm wiggled close, in sequins adorned,
Said, "Let's have a contest, the best will be sworn!"
The daffodils laughed, with bellies like drums,
"We'll make you our judge, come dance! Don't be glum!"

So gardens evolve into musical plays,
With daffodils laughing on bright sunny days.
Just one little shake from a breeze's sweet kiss,
Turns a field into fun—it's nature's pure bliss!

Chorus of the Wildflowers

In the meadow's embrace, wildflowers unite,
With petals like paint, such a colorful sight.
They sway in the breeze, sing a whimsical tune,
"We're the rave of the grass! Let's all meet at noon!"

The buttercups giggled, all yellow and bright,
"We make sunshine glow; we're pure delight!"
While poppies chimed in, all fiery and bold,
"We've stories to share, and they never get old!"

Then came the tall thistle, with spines oh so sharp,
"I can dance like no other! Just hear my loud harp!"
The other blooms chuckled, "Your moves aren't so suave,
But we love your enthusiasm, you plant pal they crave!"

From daisies to clovers, they harmonized fun,
Under the rays of the warm golden sun.
Nature's sweet chorus, so vibrant and free,
A wildflower jam, suitable for glee!

Sonnet of the Serene Succulents

Amongst the rocks where the sun kisses dew,
Succulents sit, all in tranquil review.
"Our leaves are a palette, in shades rich and bold,
We shimmer like jewels, in the sun's golden fold!"

With laughter, they ponder the rainclouds up high,
"So fickle they are, always passing us by!"
One cactus piped up, "We drink with such grace,
A sip every season—now that's our ace!"

In this succulent tale of the dry and the sweet,
Their humor's as fresh as their juices, a treat.
But potted they ponder, in friends' little homes,
"It's cozy and fun, but sometimes, we moan!"

So here's to the leafy, the spiky, the dear,
In gardens or windows, their laughter we hear.
A sonnet of stillness, where all plants belong,
In the company of greens, we cannot go wrong!

Songs of the Saplings

Tiny trees in a dance, so spry,
Swinging branches, reaching high.
A squirrel waltzes, what a sight,
Under leaves, they start a fight.

Roots quibble, 'Who's the best?'
While bees buzz in their stylish vest.
Sunbeams giggle, tickling bark,
As shadows play around the park.

Frolicking ferns in a swirl,
Spreading joy as they twirl.
Nurtured by the gentle rain,
Leaves burst forth, not one in vain.

Nature's chuckle all around,
In this merry plant-filled ground.
Join the jest, come take a look,
In this leafy storybook!

Notes from the Nightshade

Under moonlight, shadows splay,
Night's green whispers in dismay.
Nightshades giggle with delight,
As fireflies dress in flick'ring light.

Clover's clumsiness steals the show,
Tripping over roots, 'Oh no!'
While lilacs hold their laughter tight,
Fading giggles, out of sight.

One cheeky vine, he starts to climb,
Interrupting all with his rhyme.
'Who needs sleep when we can sway?',
Says the daisy in her play!

So join the fun, beneath the stars,
Dancing plants and buzzing czars.
In this wild and wacky spree,
Nightshade boasts, 'Come dance with me!'

Elegy for the Elderflower

Elderflower, a tale so sweet,
With petals soft and sprightly feet.
But bees, oh my, they just can't wait,
For nectar feasts on a floral plate.

Once a bloomer, proud and fine,
Now tangled up in a vine.
'What happened here?' the rosebud cried,
As bees buzzed, no place to hide.

Faded blooms and whispering winds,
Elderflower's story begins.
He laughs aloud, though moments past,
Memories dance, yet they won't last.

So raise a toast, let spirits soar,
For every petal, there's always more.
In gardens wild, we'll sing and sigh,
Elderflower waves, 'Goodbye, oh my!'

Aroma of Awakened Gardens

Morning wakes with a jest so bold,
Petunias shout, 'We break the mold!'
Cacti chuckle in sun's warm glow,
As lilacs spill secrets, row by row.

The daisies wear their polka dots,
While tulips boast in sunny spots.
'Come! Smell the joy!' the garden sings,
Where every flower has silly wings.

Sass of sage, mischief of thyme,
Herbs in a giggle, suddenly rhyme.
Sunflowers wave with cheeky grins,
In this garden where the laughter spins.

Whimsical breezes carry the sound,
Of nature's humor, all around.
So join the fun, let your heart share,
In this fragrant place, without a care!

Vibrations of the Verdant Vines

In the garden where the plants all sway,
The vines are dancing, come what may.
They twist and twirl, a leafy show,
Competing for the sun's warm glow.

With each green leaf, a story's told,
Of mishaps grand and adventures bold.
A snail once tried to win a race,
But got distracted by a tasty place.

The flowers giggle at the clumsy bee,
Who bumbled 'round the old oak tree.
"Keep calm!" they cheer, "You're doing great!"
But off he flies, his tiny fate.

The breeze joins in with a gentle laugh,
As petals dance and take a bow on behalf.
In this lively world, with friends so dear,
Nature's humor brings us cheer.

Petals in the Breeze

Petals flutter like a comic troupe,
Performing for the butterflies in a loop.
They puff their cheeks and strike a pose,
As the wind laughs and gently blows.

A dandelion's wish, a joke to share,
As seeds scatter here and everywhere.
"Did you hear the one about the rose?"
He told it poorly, but everyone knows.

A tulip tried to dance in style,
But tripped on roots and fell worthwhile.
Laughter erupted from the grasses near,
As groundhogs chuckled, their joy sincere.

In the floral circus where laughter reigns,
Even the weeds are breaking chains.
So come take part, let the fun begin,
With petals in the breeze, the jesters win.

Rhythms of the Rain-kissed Blooms

Raindrops tap like a drummer's beat,
Creating rhythms for the blooms' retreat.
Each petal dances, in puddles they splash,
A floral fiesta, a vibrant bash.

A daisy spun around with glee,
Until it tangled in a bumblebee.
"Excuse me, friend!" the bee did buzz,
"You're blocking my groove, that's just not fuzz!"

A marigold joked with humor fine,
"Laugh! Life's too short for a pitiful line."
As raindrops giggled on green leaf tips,
The flowers strutted their colorful flips.

So let it rain, and let it pour,
For the blooms' laughter we can't ignore.
In this garden where joy resumes,
We dance to the rhythms of the rain-kissed blooms.

Serenade of the Sunflower

In fields where sunflowers stand so tall,
They're singing loudly, one and all.
A chorus bright, with faces to the sun,
Their melody swells, oh what fun!

With seeds of wisdom, they share their tale,
Of a hungry squirrel who set out to trail.
He climbed so high for just one bite,
But slipped right down, what a funny sight!

"Hey look over here!" a blossom beams,
"Let's form a band and follow our dreams!"
As bees join in, a buzzing tune,
A sunflower symphony beneath the moon.

So sway and spin, let laughter flow,
In this sunny dance, we're stealing the show.
Life's a serenade, come join the parade,
Where sunflowers sing and beaming hearts cascade.

The Tulip's Tale

A tulip once wore a fancy hat,
Said, "I'm known for my beauty, imagine that!"
With petals so bright, it danced in the breeze,
But tripped on a bee and fell with a wheeze.

It tried to impress a rose, oh so red,
But lost all its charm when it bumped its head.
"Dear bee, lend a hand, I feel so absurd!"
The bee buzzed with laughter, clutching a nerd.

The tulip declared, "I'm still quite a sight!"
But the daffodils giggled, oh what a fright!
In gardens and fields, with laughter they play,
A tale of a tulip who flopped on the way.

So if you should trip while prancing about,
Just laugh it away, and dance—never pout!
For flowers may stumble, but joy will prevail,
Just like our friend in this silly tale.

Ballad of the Bonsai

There once was a bonsai, so small and spry,
Claimed it could levitate—oh, my oh my!
It wobbled and jiggled, a comical sight,
With roots in a bowl, it took off in flight.

Its friends, the daisies, all rolled on the ground,
"You can't float like us; you'll soon tumble down!"
But the bonsai just giggled, "I'll show you my tricks!"
Then fell from its pot, doing cartwheeling flips.

In a whirl and a twirl, it ricocheted round,
Bouncing off tulips that giggled and frowned.
"Oh, bonsai, dear buddy, your stunts are absurd!"
But laughter erupted, not one puffed a word.

In the end, it stood proud, not a scratch on its pride,
With friends all around, it savored the ride.
So the moral, my friends, is not loss, but some fun,
For even a bonsai can shine like the sun.

Fluttering Ferns

In a forest so lush, where the ferns like to sway,
They danced through the night, and played without pay.
"Catch us if you can!" they teased with delight,
But stumbled on roots, what a comical sight.

A fern said, "I bet you can't jump like me!"
Then tripped on a twig—oh, what a spree!
The mushrooms all chuckled, and rolled on the floor,
While the daisies all gasped, shouted, "Do it once more!"

With laughter contagious, they spun and they twirled,
The ferns led the charge, in a whimsical world.
When one took a leap, the others would cheer,
Saying, "Ferns can be silly! Now bring on the beer!"

So next time you frolic through nature's embrace,
Remember those ferns and their humorous chase.
For even in gardens where the green comes alive,
A dance with a giggle helps all of us thrive.

Chorus of the Carnations

The carnations convened for a song and a dance,
"Let's celebrate life! Come on, take a chance!"
But one spritely bloom yawned wide and slipped loose,
Fell smack on a tulip—oh what a ruse.

They harmonized sweetly, their petals on show,
But a daisy chimed in, "Hey, don't upstage the flow!"
With petals a-twirl, they took to the floor,
And danced all together, hind legs and all four.

A bumblebee buzzed in to join the fun,
"With a beat like this, we'll shine like the sun!"
But misstepped in rhythm and flew into leaves,
Down crashed a rose, blushing with mighty grieves.

Yet laughter erupted, the roses all winked,
"In gardens of bloom, it's laughter we think!"
So they sang through the fields, with joy and with cheer,
A chorus of flowers, forever sincere.

The Sage's Soliloquy

Oh sage on the shelf, so bright and so bold,
You tell me my secrets, but your leaves are too old.
With wisdom you sprinkle, but what can you brew?
I'm hoping for tea, yet it smells more like glue.

In haughty attire, you dance by the pot,
With every herb's tale, I'm forgetting the plot.
You chuckle at thorns while I struggle to prune,
Oh sage, bring your laughter beneath the full moon.

A sprinkle of humor, a pinch of delight,
Your leaves are my compass, guiding me right.
I'll stir up a stew, but oh dear, what's this?
Your jokes are so fragrant, I can't help but miss!

So sage, let us jest, with a grin ear to ear,
For life is a garden, let's plant it with cheer.
Together we'll thrive, both you and I know,
It's the laughter in leaves that helps us to grow.

A Symphony of Sap

Beneath the old tree, the sap starts to sing,
It's sticky and sweet, just like joy in the spring.
The squirrels gather round for a syrupy feast,
With a cough and a choke, they'll be stuck to the beast.

As drips turn to gurgles, the chaos unfurls,
With sap on their tails, the poor squirrels in swirls.
They giggle and wiggle, a quirky ballet,
While the tree taps his toes to a sap-tapping sway.

Let's gather the critters, for a dance in the bark,
With laughter and sap, we'll stay out until dark.
The frogs croak in rhythm, the birds chirp a tune,
A symphony of sap beneath the bright moon.

So raise your glasses high, let's toast to the goo,
To the messy adventures in nature's fond brew.
For in every sweet drop, there's joy on the rise,
And laughter, like sap, is a precious surprise.

The Wisteria's Whisper

Oh wisteria blooms, with your purple cascade,
You tickle the window, a delicate parade.
You whisper sweet nothings, but oh, what a tease,
My neighbors just shriek, 'That's too much to please!'

With flowers so ample, you sway in the breeze,
Entangled in mischief, you dance with such ease.
As you dangle and twirl in the afternoon light,
It's hard not to giggle at your floral delight.

You wrap round the trellis, with humor and grace,
Leaving bees in a tizzy, they buzz in a race.
Together we chuckle at nature's grand show,
For a wisteria's whisper is a laugh-down below.

So let's paint the garden with colors so bright,
With flowers like jokes that bring pure delight.
Dear wisteria, friend, in you I confide,
With laughter and petals, let's joyously glide.

Gardenside Reverie

In the gardenside realm where the daisies conspire,
The gnomes hold a meeting 'round the old bonfire.
With hats that are crooked and gossip galore,
Their punchlines are plenty, they always want more.

The roses sit prim, with a giggle or two,
While dandelions blow, making wishes come true.
They chuckle and cheer as the petals take flight,
In a whimsical whirlwind, what a sight! What a sight!

The violets tease, with a wink and a nudge,
Promising blooms while they absolutely judge.
The secrets of soil, they giggle and spread,
As the tulips all whisper what should go unsaid.

So come join the laughter, the mirth and the cheer,
In the gardenside reverie, there's nothing to fear.
With flowers as witnesses, let joy intertwine,
In this raucous garden, where all is divine.

Verses from the Vines

In the vineyard, grapes do prance,
They dance and twirl, not missing a chance.
One said to the other, "Let's not be wine!"
"We'll just grape together and call it divine!"

A clumsy vine tripped, oh what a sight,
Fell over a fence, gave the bugs quite a fright.
The sunflowers giggled, in their golden hues,
"You've got to be smoother, you're stepping on shoes!"

The Flower's Elysium

Petunias wear hats, they're quite the scene,
With petals like ribbons, so bright and keen.
They laugh at daisies, so plain and sweet,
"Look at us, we're the garden's elite!"

Roses tell jokes, but thorns get them down,
"We're prickly comedians, with crowns but no crown!"
The lilacs chimed in, with a lavender hue,
"What do you expect? We're just blooming with you!"

Cadence of the Colorful Canopy

Leaves whispered secrets in the soft breeze,
"Did you see how that branch nearly fell from the trees?"
The maple said, "Dance, oh let's sway and fly!"
While the willow replied, "Only if we try!"

A crow perched near, with a chuckle so fair,
"What's with the gossip? Does anyone care?"
"We're just having fun, take a leaf and join!"
"Oh all right! I'll follow the grapevines' groin!"

Aria of the Alpine Flora

Mossy rocks peek, from the snow and the sleet,
"Let's throw a ball, with a mountain retreat!"
Daisies and violets in snow boots so neat,
They twirled in the cold, skipped around on their feet.

Lupines made chai, served on silvery trays,
"Get cozy, my friends! It's a chilly bouquet."
The laughter rang true, mingled with a tune,
While cozying up in the glimmering moon.

Chronicle of the Cacti

In the desert's dry embrace, they stand quite tall,
With prickly arms that wave, saying, "Come one, come all!"
They hold a party, just a spiny affair,
But guests beware, for hugs could lead to a scare!

Underneath the blazing sun, they sip on cool drinks,
While giggling with the lizards, oh, how their humor stinks!
Each cactus wears a hat, made of sand and sun,
And every spiky laugh is like a little pun!

When the wind blows softly, they dance all around,
Their shadows shuffle lightly, not making a sound.
The cholla's doing tango, the saguaro's in a spin,
Who knew that prickly plants could have such fun within?

As the stars twinkle brightly, they sing a spiky tune,
The desert's music plays, beneath a silver moon.
So if you're feeling lonely, and your day feels flat,
Just find a cactus party—now that's a real chat!

The Rose's Requiem

Oh, what a tale the rose has to tell,
With petals so red, she's a floral belle.
But beware her whispers, sharp and sly,
For every sweet laugh hides a thorny lie!

Under the moonlight, she held a grand ball,
Invited all flowers, the big and the small.
With daisies in dresses and tulips in ties,
The cacophony of giggles made petals rise!

But just when the fun reached a raucous peak,
The rose slipped off her stem, oh how unique!
With a flop and a twist, she landed with flair,
Now she's spinning stories from her patch of air!

Though her bright hue gleams, she laughs at her plight,
Dancing in the moonlight, feeling quite light.
She might be a thorny dame, but still, she knows,
Life's most fragrant moments come from the fun that grows!

Thorns and Tones

In a garden of giggles, a thistle took stage,
With a rap full of rhythm and a hint of rage.
He claimed he was cool, though prickly and rough,
And said, "Watch me shine; I'm tough but enough!"

The daisies chuckled, their voices aglow,
While the violets blushed, putting on quite a show.
Each flower in bloom had a part in the play,
But that old thistle boasted, night turned into day!

Then from behind, the lilies crept in,
With silky smooth moves, giving him a spin.
"Dear friend," they crooned, "Your thorns don't define,
Join our merry dance, and we'll all intertwine!"

So together they jived, with laughter and dance,
In the garden's sweet glow, they took a wild chance.
Thorns and tones entwined, a union so grand,
Who says sharp edges can't lend a helping hand?

Hymn of the Herbaceous

In a patch of green, where the basil does sway,
Lives a band of herb friends, who brighten the day.
With cilantro's quick wit and thyme's gentle laugh,
They share silly puns—they're the garden's staff!

Once a week they gather for their herbivore jam,
Mint is the DJ, stirring up the slam!
"Parsley, let's groove!" cries the bold rosemary,
And together they sway, an herbal ballet!

Chives love to twirl with their frilly green crowns,
While the sage tells a story that turns wild frowns.
Each sprout, each leaf, brings laughter anew,
In the herbaceous choir, chaos ensues!

So next time you see them, give a little cheer,
For herbs have great fun, and they spread it near.
With laughter and flavor, they spice up the scene,
Join the hymn of the herbaceous, let's all be green!

The Ballad of the Blossoming Boughs

In the grove where flowers dance,
Silly bees take every chance.
Blossoms giggle, sway, and twirl,
While butterflies play, swoop, and whirl.

Oh, the roses wear a shade of glee,
Winking at the bumblebee.
Tulips prance in colors bright,
Pretending they are stars at night.

The daisies tell the sun to stay,
While violets shout, "Hip-hip-hooray!"
Nature's jesters, pure delight,
Making merry from day to night.

Underneath the leafy crown,
Laughter echoes all around.
In this realm where flora reigns,
Even feuds are just for laughs and gains.

Reveries in the Rosy Retreat

In the shade of the blooming rose,
Petals whisper all their woes.
"Why do humans stop and stare?"
"Do they think we're debonair?"

Carnations clash in playful jest,
Poking fun at nature's best.
"Watch that tulip, oh so proud,
Thinks it's better than the crowd!"

Lilies laugh at their own scent,
"Do we make bees feel content?"
While ferns shake their fronds in glee,
"Stay away from our tea party!"

In the garden, jesters play,
Flora's humor on display.
Taking pride in every joke,
In this retreat, laughter's no hoax.

Petals in the Moonlight

Underneath the silver glow,
Flowers wear their finest show.
Daisies toss their heads in cheer,
While nightingales croon songs sincere.

The moonlight casts a funny line,
As sunflowers try to shine.
"Hey moon, let's see who's more bright!"
Laughter echoes through the night.

Jasmine winks and whispers low,
"Let's make the stars dance to and fro!"
Petals prance on gentle breeze,
Sharing giggles with the trees.

In this evening's cozy shroud,
Every flower sings aloud.
Under blossoms, joy takes flight,
In the garden, what a sight!

Secrets of the Greenhouse

Inside the glass, the secrets bloom,
Potting soil and garden gloom.
Cacti poke with prickly pride,
While mint leaves spread their jokes worldwide.

The herbs might snicker, soft and sage,
On all the drama of the stage.
"Parsley thinks it's quite an expert,
But we all know it's just a flirt!"

Tomatoes blush at every glare,
"Should we dress up or just wear air?"
In this greenhouse, life's a jest,
Every plant thinks it's the best.

With laughter growing day by day,
Every leaf has something to say.
In the soil, giggles intertwine,
Nature's humor will always shine.

Prose of Petunias

In the garden, blooms reside,
Petunias, oh how they glide!
With colors bright and scents so sweet,
They dance around on tiny feet.

One petunia wore a hat so grand,
Another tried to play in the sand.
They giggled loud, took off in flight,
Chasing butterflies, pure delight.

A bee came buzzing, oh what a fright,
They shrieked and swayed with all their might.
With petals flapping like a cape,
They vowed they'd never let him escape!

So here they laugh, they sing with glee,
These chatty blooms, so wild and free.
In their prose of petals, fun is key,
In this merry garden, just wait and see!

A Rhubarb Reverie

In the patch where rhubarb grows,
A tale of jam and pies bestows.
With leafy crowns and stems so red,
They plotted sweet treats in their head.

One rhubarb said, "Let's start a band!"
"With pie crusts, we'll be in high demand!"
But when they tried to make a tune,
They sounded like a grumpy raccoon.

So they danced instead, in silly hops,
Flinging leaves, that made quite the plops.
They twirled and rolled across the ground,
Creating chaos in leaps and bounds.

"Oh dear!" cried one, "This is too fun!"
"Let's invite the carrots for a run!"
The garden echoed with laughter bright,
A rhubarb revelry all night!

Harmony of the Hyacinth

In a garden bright, the hyacinth sway,
With scents so sweet, they steal the day.
They gather round with friends in bloom,
Spreading laughter, filling the room.

"Let's sing a song!" chirped one with grace,
"Of buzzing bees and every place!"
But off-key they were, what a fright,
They turned the dusk into a night.

With petals shaking, causing a fuss,
One tripped and fell in the garden bus!
"Help me up!" he cried with glee,
As laughter echoed from every tree.

"Let's party now, we'll have a ball!"
"Who needs a tune? Let's have a brawl!"
With giggles and jests, they danced away,
In harmony that brightened the day!

The Climbing Clematis

Up the trellis, the clematis climbs,
Telling tales in twisted rhymes.
With every twist, they giggle and soar,
"Watch me touch the sky!" they swore.

A friend called out, "I'll race you high!"
One leaf shouted, "I'll surely fly!"
With whirls and twirls, they went uphill,
But tangled up, they lost their thrill.

"Help! I'm stuck!" one called in dread,
"As leaves are laughing, I'm seeing red!"
Then suddenly they all burst free,
And shared a chuckle, just wait and see!

Together now, they soared in style,
Climbing higher, all with a smile.
In the garden where laughter is free,
The clematis shines, as wild as can be!

Swaying in the Sun

In the garden, things do sway,
Dancing weeds, come out to play.
Sunshine tickles every sprout,
While the bugs just bounce about.

Petunias giggle, tulips tease,
Spinning stories with the breeze.
Daisies tell the sun their dreams,
Their laughter flows in golden beams.

A rose turns red, with quite the flair,
While violets whisper, 'Who cares?'
The marigold sings goofy tunes,
As butterflies float, wearing loons.

We all sway, let's not be shy,
With clovers hopping high and dry.
Join the fun, the merry run,
In this garden soaked in sun.

The Cleansing Clover

A lucky clover, fresh and green,
Claims it's the cleanest I have seen.
It scrubs my thoughts with gentle glee,
An awkward plant, it loves to be!

With four leaves spread, it makes a mess,
Polishing my mind—no stress!
'Just a pinch of dirt,' it says with pride,
'And watch your worries take a ride!'

Each grubby thought it can erase,
While dodging ladybugs in a race.
'This is how I clean,' it beams,
'With laughter echoing in the streams!'

So if you're feeling all a-foul,
Let clover take its cleansing prowl.
A quick little shake and giggle too,
Your thoughts will sparkle, fresh as dew!

The Heart of the Heliotrope

A heliotrope, with heart so bright,
Follows the sun with pure delight.
It whispers secrets, sweet and fine,
   To giggling bees all in a line.

With petals soft, it takes the stage,
   Bowing gracefully, like a sage.
It tells the daisies, 'Make some noise!,'
While painting skies with perfect poise.

The sun dips low, it laughs and twirls,
Chasing shadows, like playful whirls.
Its fragrance tickles, makes you grin,
   Like a little jester pulling you in.

   In the garden, it wins the prize,
For charming hearts and brightening skies.
   Oh, heliotrope, you silly sprite,
With your sunny dances, what a sight!

A Musing of Marrows

In a patch where veggies grow,
Marrows dream of stealing the show.
With big round faces, looking sly,
They plot to bounce and twist, oh my!

Swaying gently on their stalks,
They giggle softly with the chocks.
'If we wear hats, will we be cool?'
Oh yes, says carrot, 'Just play the fool!'

Zucchini joins the stellar cast,
Swapping tales, so unsurpassed.
A vegetable ball, oh what a scene,
As marrows twirl in vivid green!

So when you see them in a row,
Don't be surprised by their frolic show.
These marrows love to laugh and dance,
In their veggie world, they take a chance.

www.ingramcontent.com/pod-product-compliance
Lightning Source LLC
Chambersburg PA
CBHW071823160426
43209CB00003B/182